A Heroine, Complete

Shauna Alderson

BookLeaf Publishing

Presentation by *BookLeaf Publishing*

Web: www.bookleafpub.com

E-mail: info@bookleafpub.com

ISBN: 9789395950695

First edition 2022

To my parents, Bess and Kevin. Love you both immensely.

ACKNOWLEDGEMENT

Huge thanks go out to all these lovely people.

To the team at BookLeaf Publishing for this opportunity.
To the East Bay Beta Readers and Writers for reminding me to write.
To Becky Wright for your support from halfway across the globe.
To Freshia Corpus for sending me funnies and motivations virtually every day.
To Emily Strong for your lifelong friendship and go-for-it attitude (hello to little Noa!).
To Mandy and Oliver for your uplifting positivity.
To my uncle, Scott Alderson, for setting the precedent (go check out his poetry collections!).
To all of my family—Bess, Kevin, Troy, Gerry, Sam, Aljohn, Elleiana, Kallina, Ricardo, Susan, and all the titas and titos I could spend an entire day writing down—for everything, but especially for wasting time with me in the best ways possible.
And to you, dear reader, for picking up this obscure little book.
Much love to you all.

PREFACE

When I was a young girl consuming children's cartoons at my grandma's house, my dream was to become the princess of the Power Rangers—or "Power Princess", for short. I wanted to be the heroine of my own life and help as many people as I could along the way. This was, of course, before Reality ensued and curled my dreams back into seeds of potentiality.

I'm sorry to tell you, reader, that we begin this collection with pain. Pain is the "inciting incident"—the event that starts the heroine on her journey of discovery. In my case, it was perfectionism in all its forms, budding from soil devoid of self-worth. But after pain comes realization and an awareness of necessary changes. Lastly, we end with the heroine complete in her power.

I feel it's important to note that I didn't write these poems in order. Healing is a cycle—some days I'm still running, and some days I'm becoming. At the end of the day, I'm not sure if I'll ever live up to the Power Princess of my youth, but I look into the future and it's ever-teeming with wonder.

I hope it is for you too.

Princess runs

How many times have I run from criticism
Stopped myself short before I could start
Hid works in progress before someone saw
And said they weren't good enough

How many times have I let myself down
Just to boost everyone else up
Hoping for a thank you, token of approval
Once they got where they needed to be

How many times have I wished I could fly
Only to tell myself that I can't
That my wings are insignificant
Compared to the winds in the sky

How many times have I made myself small
Just to avoid being a visible target
Easier to hear my own ruthless critic
Than unwelcome judgments of others

No matter how many times before
I promise myself now
Never again

See me

I see myself
As a small child
Standing in the downstairs den
TV blaring
Parent's eyes glued
The surroundings of my memory
A dark irritated red
Downstairs family room
Computer thrumming
Brother's eyes glued
The texture of my memory
Harsh carpet on sensitive feet

Standing alone
I see myself
A distance away, in between
Couch and computer
Parent and brother
Looming on throne-like seats
I dare not ask them to
Look my way
In case a snapping tone
Breaks the peace
Their time is king

A small child like me
Should not be seen

Changemaker

I'm a witness
To how it's torn holes in walls
Opened wounds in hearts
Demolished years of building
In a single eruption
Fearful fact
That all carry such fury
Such capacity

I've tried not to wield it
But it escapes in increments
Tried not to express it
But I stumble on its yearning
For freedom, this caged phoenix
Longs to be allowed
To fly in the rawness
And humanness
Of the moment
Tearing down the defunct
Replacing it with workings
And for once, being sincere

Will I listen?
Anger has only ever
Brought me trouble

Coping

I tend toward the melancholic
Blame my parents, both workaholics
No one home to raise my spirits
Expectation layered with regrets

From the outside, speaking genuine
Game of hide-and-seek, I win
Obfuscating what lies within
Starry night, the light has thinned

Don't be surprised to discover this
Side of me's too introspective
The contemplators I identify with
Know that darkness lurks in crevices

Go on, tell me to be positive
And live the life I'm meant to live
I'll still lean toward melancholic
Not by choice, but via habit

I hope for the day I finally "get it"
Waking up feeling appreciated
But until then, let there be sadness
Let light be born in the purest darkness

Weight of the world

The weight of the world on your shoulders,
Mother
How it pains me to watch you suffer
I can't ease the strain when you're the one
Who holds it there in the first place
We've tried to chip away at it
But you protect your burden
Like a newborn babe on your back
Afraid things will fall apart if you're no longer

Responsible
For everything
All the time

I wish you would let yourself relax
Let yourself recuperate
Until then, I can only stand by
As you heft more invisible weights
Onto your aching back

The weight of the world on your shoulders
Mother, I learned that from you

My first child

Her name is Brokenness
My Baby B.
First-time parent still figuring it out
Is it ok to give her space?
Or should I tuck her back in?
Down down down we go

I tell her to hush now
That's what parents do
Children always crying
What is it this time?
Please go back to bed
A new day will greet us soon

Baby B. will not be consoled
Stop it already
Time to suck it up like the rest of us
I've tried everything and
You're getting in my way
I've got so many things to do

Now she doesn't like her crib
Too many bars—for her protection, you know
Don't want her falling out and causing a scene
What would friends think of my parenting

I need her to be good
She'll understand when she's older

Growing too fast
Can't bottle-feed her anymore
I've given her everything I have
But she's wanting more
You call this gratitude?
Well, you can just leave

I never needed you anyway
I don't

Brokenness came back today
I recognized myself in her
Don't know why I never did before
We grab a coffee and catch up
It's been such a long time
You have so much to tell me

Mask for sale

Heavily discounted
Trying to get rid of it
Has a beautiful smile
        All the while
Going through sadness
Always laughs at your jokes
        Never pokes
At your opinions
Always keeps the peace
        Never speaks
Out of turn
A true blank face
        Can't trace
Its own concerns
Great for parties and gatherings
Crowd pleaser for sure
Mask for sale
DM me for details

Princess begun

How long
I ask myself
How long until I can fly
Until something shifts
Until I feel I've made it
How long until the cocoon bursts
And sets me soaring
Upon this vast exciting world

A fretful sigh escapes
As I climb
So busy looking up
That I forget to look down
View the ground
And celebrate how far
I've already come

Foreign languages

Odd, isn't it
How so many people speak through
Words I don't understand
Thoughts of a different palate
Concepts I cannot grasp
Because of their sound
I've tried learning some
But it confounds me
How much there is to discover
In my very own tongue

Astonishing how many people live out
Truths I can't understand
Meanings in a different palette
Contexts I cannot fathom
Because of my background
I've traveled before
But still it confounds me
How much there is left
In my own world to explore

Maybe someday
Once I've touched the stars in a grain of sand
The universal in the individual
I'll fully understand

Compass

I had many dreams once
A bucket list to tick off
Places to see and things to acquire
I've reached a few
And oh, how disappointing
After it's yours
To still feel the same as before
No emotional shift
Despite the check-marked tick
Could it be that the dreams were curtains
And what actually matters
Is the emotion resting behind
What the dream meant to you

Expression

I wondered before
Why artists always revisited
The same material
Time and time again
Now I try to write the words
And they're never complete
Always another facet to catch the light
Another nuance to investigate
I try to capture
The effervescent essence
Of my whole emotions
Never perfect
These almost-truths
Trying their best to be seen and known
To unveil the heart
The walls come tumbling but
The foundations remain

I no longer wonder why
Artists rinse and repeat
Time and time again
Because a million words will
Never do
To fully encapsulate
This energy-in-motion

Rulebreaker

They told me don't be naive
Or you'll get bruised
Don't rely on faith
You'll be disappointed
Don't be a dreamer
Since they never live
But I no longer listen

They told me don't be an artist
You need to eat
Don't be sensitive
Or you'll get hurt
Don't overreach
The sun will burn
But I no longer listen

They told me I'm no healer
Human, not divine
Better wait for the Son
Someone more than I
To flick on the light
But why should I
When I no longer listen

They told me how I should be
To flavour the "be yourself, be yourself"
Now I show them who I am
By breaking all the rules
I no longer listen to
Because freedom is divine

Impetus

The moment when
The wave hits the beach
You realize it's been building
This entire time
In the great deep ocean
Unseen and unfelt
Building and building
Until it breaks over the sands
Sharing its knowledge
Its purpose
Its purity
With anyone who wishes to receive
Will you accept?
It's never too late
Another wave will come to life
In just a moment

Calling

I can say you came out of nowhere
But the truth is you've been pulling me
Since before I can remember
Calling me to go deeper
Farther than any safety I know
Away from plans I tried to make work
You knew they wouldn't, didn't you
You always knew I'd come around
I'm in your hands now
Please don't let me down

Princess becomes

One of my first memories
A run-in with my guardian angel
I jumped too high off the stairs
Fell gently as a feather
Dream or not
It was real to me

Golden wings around my body
Protecting and shielding
Feathers soft and warm
I hold them there myself
Imagined or not
They are real to me

Golden light at my disposal
Running through my fingertips
Reaching through me to reality
I create from this holy place
Naive or not
God is real to me

And I am ready

Moving on

Wishing you the best
I'm sorry how it ended
But I couldn't let you hurt me
Without defending
I'm sorry how it went, didn't mean
To say those things without thinking
Thought I'd thought them through
But now I see how blind I'd been
I'd take it all back if I could

Listening to what you've been up to
These days
Looks like you're doing well
I hope it's not a front
Hope it's the truth
Don't want to be
Holding you back
After this long
I'm doing well too

Present day

Letter to myself
Goes something like this
From the moment you came into being
Maybe long before then
You were loved
Not for what you do
Or earn or accomplish
But for being
                    Present
In the lives around you
You are a
                    Present
Bestowed to the world
By the powers above
And I will celebrate you
Even when no one else does

You are loved, my self
Not for what you do
Or earn or accomplish
But for the many
                    Gifts
You bring to the world
For you are a
                    Gift

No one else can give
And I will appreciate you
Even when no one else does
Because you've already earned it
And in my eyes, you are love

Reframe

You would tell me
Whenever I hit the wrong note
Struck the wrong chord
In a booming voice
That all could hear
Everyone knew
Whenever I made a mistake

And so I was afraid
Of learning new songs
Of pausing the flow
Of practicing at all
Because beauty
Is supposed to be played smoothly

I stopped trying for many years
As you know

But if I look back
At how you always sat on the couch
Whenever I sat at the keys
Always listening
Whenever I practiced
It’s because you loved hearing me play
That’s why you told me what was wrong

Not because you were judging
But because you were supporting me
In your own way

Now I choose to remember
How you always sat on the couch
Not to tell me I'm wrong
But just waiting to sing along

Small wonders

Sweet perfume of a blooming cactus
Majesty of the galaxy above
This is what I remember most
From a trip to somewhere new
The small wonders
No great words
Or greater achievements
Have left me as breathless
As the stars holding each other's light
Softly among the blooms of night
I remember an instance
Of unadulterated laughter
Couldn't stop the sheer joy
Couldn't tell you why
Just that it was easy
And years later, I can't recall
What I said or did on that trip
In between the laughing and ogling
At small wonders
In their grandest moments

Soulknown

The moment I met you
I knew you
Behind the mischievous glint in your eye
Lay the depths of the universe
Its miracles coming into focus
Like a mirror
Something as deep and familiar
To me as my own reflection
Eons of history
Lifetimes spent side by side
I knew you then
I've found you again

You say time only separated us
To grow unique petals
No layers to peel away
When we know each other's core
Time to explore
What new growth we can flower together
As spring smiles on us again

Shooting stars in orbit

Every rotation of the earth marks a day
Every circle around the sun, a year
The earth does not stop on its path
Even when it finishes one or two
Though it is wholly complete
Its perpetual purpose
Keeps it afloat
On a river no one else can see

The earth cannot wonder why
A year from now, it faces the same stars
A shame and a blessing
Unlike humankind
It cannot think or dream
Past the cycle of the galaxy

So on this guided wandering
That often returns to the beginning
To face the same familiar stars
I know I have not backtracked
I know I am complete
And my purpose here
Keeps me afloat
On a river heading out to sea

www.ingramcontent.com/pod-product-compliance
Lightning Source LLC
Chambersburg PA
CBHW062109140826
49812CB00058B/1072
9789395950695